EVERYDAY

WITNESS

"Authentic evangelizers live Sr. Theresa Rickard's seven habits seemingly without much thought, but in fact they adopt them through intentional reflection in a community of faith. Rickard's stories of ordinary Christians living holy lives illustrate missionary discipleship as being relatable and attainable. We too can be disciples and disciple-makers, using our unique gifts. I am deeply grateful for this inspiring work."

Diane Kledzik
Director for Marriage and Family Life
Diocese of St. Petersburg

"Sr. Terry Rickard is the Stephen Covey of highly effective habits for a joyful, Christian journey. Practicing what she preaches, her captivating stories and prayers elicit a tear and a chuckle for a fervent Christian seeking to share the faith."

Rev. Anthony Randazzo
Pastor of Holy Trinity Parish
Westfield, New Jersey

"Sr. Terry Rickard's *Everyday Witness* is like being right in the middle of a small faith-sharing group. Carefully chosen stories are presented to teach the reader that sharing faith is not very difficult if we simply stop and listen to stories shared by faith-filled people. It's practical wisdom in a user-friendly format. This little book is fantastic!"

Theodore J. Musco
Secretary for Evangelization and Catechesis
Diocese of Brooklyn

"*Everyday Witness* is an excellent book that weaves together a beautiful tapestry of scripture and everyday life. Inspirational stories about women and men of faith remind us of God's abiding presence in both the ups and downs of life. The appendix features two wonderful features, tips for sharing your faith story and cultivating a sense of witness in your parish, to help live and give witness to our Catholic faith."

Rev. Jeremiah Browne
South Africa Coordinator
RENEW Africa

"As Church we need to reintroduce and awaken the real meaning of sharing our faith without complicating the process. In the words of Sr. Terry Rickard, O.P., 'Many of us long to share what we believe so that others might also believe.' Rickard introduces beginners to faith sharing in its truest form. Her seven simple habits are exactly the tools I have been seeking for small group faith–sharing participants. This book keeps the experience from becoming a complicated process and is a wonderful experience that, in time, we grow into. I am especially fond of the third habit: 'Preach from the pulpit of your life.' The way we live speaks clearly about who God is for us and for those we meet along the paths of Christian discipleship."

Sr. Linda LaMagna, C.C.W.
Coordinator, Evangelization Office
Diocese of Altoona–Johnstown

EVERYDAY

7 Simple Habits

WITNESS

FOR Sharing YOUR Faith

THERESA RICKARD, O.P.

AVE MARIA PRESS AVE Notre Dame, Indiana

Founded in 1865, Ave Maria Press is a ministry of the United States Province of Holy Cross.

www.avemariapress.com

Paperback: ISBN-13 978-1-59471-923-3

E-book: ISBN-13 978-1-59471-924-0

Cover background © Lost & Taken.

Cover and text design by Brianna Dombo.

Printed and bound in the United States of America.

Library of Congress Cataloging-in-Publication Data
Names: Rickard, Theresa, author.
Title: Everyday witness : 7 simple habits for sharing your faith / Theresa Rickard, O.P.
Description: Notre Dame, IN : Ave Maria Press, 2020.
Identifiers: LCCN 2019020169 (print) | ISBN 9781594719233 (pbk.)
Subjects: LCSH: Evangelistic work--Catholic Church. | Witness bearing (Christianity) | Spiritual life--Catholic Church. | Christian life--Catholic authors.
Classification: LCC BX2347.4 .R53 2020 (print) | LCC BX2347.4 (ebook) | DDC 248/.5--dc23
LC record available at https://lccn.loc.gov/2019020169
LC ebook record available at https://lccn.loc.gov/2019981488

TABLE OF CONTENTS

INTRODUCTION

MORE THAN WORDS

Have you ever been deeply moved by a friend's story of experiencing God at work in her life? Have you been impressed or even awed by a fellow parishioner telling about meeting Jesus for the first time, or the time he felt the Holy Spirit urging him to act in one way or another? Stories of religious faith are interesting to those of us who believe, aren't they? So many of us find God and talk about God in our everyday lives and we are indeed called to do just that—to give witness to our values, beliefs, and religious commitments by telling others about what we believe and how we meet God in ordinary experiences at home, in our place of work or school, or while running errands. And we crave the skills and courage to speak about God present in the precious moments of our lives, such as the death of a loved one or the birth of a baby.

Sharing the realities of God acting in our lives has the power to help those with whom we share a passing moment, an ongoing activity, or even a lifetime, see God present and working in their own lives. As most church ministers will confirm in a heartbeat, seekers and believers alike need to hear the faith stories of others in order to encounter Christ or to encounter him anew. In this little book, you will learn about seven simple habits to help you give humble witness to your faith and point others to the way of Jesus. Simple habits of sharing God's activity in your everyday life will make God's presence more readily felt among the people with whom you frequently interact. These habits of word and action will help you pass on the richness of our Catholic faith to your children, grandchildren, family, friends, coworkers, and neighbors. This book, put simply, will guide you to become an everyday witness to the power of our loving God.

Authentic and humble witness to Christ transforms hearts, giving people the meaningful ability to reorder their lives. Throughout my own life, I have been blessed by many people who have shared powerful faith stories with me. They have pointed me to life in Christ as the meaning of our lives. Faith stories told with simplicity and lived with authenticity make God recognizable to others. The recollection, review, and retelling of our God-moments—those specific, powerful moments of knowing deep in our hearts that we have encountered God—deepens our relationship with God. We come to understand and appreciate more deeply how God works in our lives.

We Catholics often struggle to share our faith, especially in words. Many of us think faith is a rather private matter, and we certainly don't want to impose our beliefs on others. Some of us altogether avoid conversations about religion in order to avoid conflict. We might simply feel inadequate when we try to talk about our faith and think it best to leave religious talk to professionals. Yet many of us have friends, family members, coworkers, and neighbors who belong to other Christian communities and who seem to feel quite at ease giving witness to their own faith.

Now, I am *not* proposing that on a regular basis you debate the existence of God or the doctrines of the Church with others. Rather, I am suggesting that you learn to engage comfortably in "God-talk"—spiritual conversations that uplift, comfort, and challenge. Many who need to hear about God do not go to church or to faith-formation programs in our parishes. The only church some people will meet is *you*. Who will pass on the faith to the next generation—to your children and grandchildren—if not you? Who will bring words of healing and messages of God's unconditional mercy to your friends and family if not you? Who will model a life based on Gospel values of charity and justice in your community, workplace, and society if not you?

In Pope Francis's exhortation on evangelization titled *The Joy of the Gospel,* he writes about giving witness to our faith while not forcing our faith on others. Evangelization is spreading the Good News of salvation in Christ, and in this important teaching document, the pope helps us learn how to evangelize. He urges us to draw people to faith by attraction and not by proselytizing, which means trying to convert another. He urges against pushing the Bible or the *Catechism of the Catholic Church* or trying overtly to steer people away from other forms of Christianity or from other religions and toward ours. The purpose of witnessing to our faith is not to muscle others into our belief system. Rather, it is to help them experience the fruits of our faith, sometimes called the fruits of the Holy Spirit: love, joy, peace, kindness, goodness, faithfulness, gentleness, and self-control. The purpose of witnessing is to introduce others to the person and way of Jesus Christ, who embodies all of these attributes.

Developing the simple habits described in this book will enable you to share your faith through attraction. Each habit begins with a verb—an action word. These seven words are simple to comprehend, if not always easy to do: *choose, be, preach, pray, listen, practice, engage.* Once you understand how these actions help you learn to talk about God and about your faith, and once you begin to practice them, you will find that they become part of your everyday way of being in this world as one who draws others to Christ. Let these words and these habits, become your rallying cry as you become an everyday witness.

In *The Joy of the Gospel*, Pope Francis writes: "People today put more trust in witnesses than in teachers, in experience than in teaching, and in life and action than in theories." The everyday witness of Christian life is the first and irreplaceable form of mission. Christ, whose mission we continue, is the witness par excellence; he is the model of all Christian witness. From the very beginning of Christianity, faith in Christ has always been spread by witness from person to person, from one loving and compassionate heart to another.

As spouses, parents, and grandparents, aunts and uncles, godparents, friends and neighbors, catechists, religious, lay parish ministers, and clergy, we are first and foremost called to be witnesses to our faith in Jesus Christ. The heart of discipleship is to proclaim Christ by words of faith, lives of joy, and acts of charity and justice. Charitable works address an immediate need, while works on behalf of justice address what actions are needed to remove that immediate need. As Pope Francis instructed a parish community at a parish on the eastern edge of Rome in early 2017, "Christian witness is done with three things: words, the heart, and the hands." These are not three distinct ways to give witness; instead, they are each a part of the whole. Just as we can't separate love of God from love of neighbor, we can't separate our words from our motives or our actions. Our whole person testifies to the goodness of our Creator. We share that goodness with our words, our hearts, and our hands. This is what it means to be a missionary disciple, a follower of Jesus Christ, called and sent to be an everyday witness to his way.

I hope the seven simple and easy-to-adapt habits shared here will help you grow comfortable in giving authentic, life-changing witness to your faith. Such witness will touch your loved ones, your neighbors, the Church, and the world, which so clearly needs the powerful Good News of love and the tender mercy of our compassionate God. Along with sharing my own thoughts about and experience of each habit for learning to witness our faith, I point you to specific biblical passages that teach us about each habit. I also tell you about someone in my own life who has witnessed to me each habit, offer guidance for self-reflection, tips for growing the habit, and prayers to open and close each chapter. My hope is that this book becomes a tool for spiritual growth and practical skill development in the Christian task of spreading the Good News of our salvation in Christ Jesus.

1.

CHOOSE JOY

Begin WITH Prayer

Therefore my heart is glad,
    and my soul rejoices;
    my body also rests secure.

You show me the path of life.
    In your presence there is fullness of
    joy;
    In your right hand are pleasures
    forevermore.

                      —Psalm 16:9, 11

Choose

First we must choose joy. We are invited to witness to the truth of what we just prayed in Psalm 16, a song of trust. We find comfort that in God's presence there is "fullness of joy." If God's presence is full joy, then when we radiate joy, we radiate God. It's simple—joy attracts, while gloom nearly always repels.

One of my favorite remarks by Pope Francis is, "Don't be a sourpuss!" Obviously, the pope has encountered more than a few Christian sourpusses in his day. His colorful and spontaneous language immediately caught the world's attention, and he included the term "sourpuss" in *The Joy of the Gospel*, where he writes: "One of the more serious temptations which stifles boldness and zeal is a defeatism which turns us into querulous and disillusioned pessimists, 'sourpusses'" (85). When Francis originally used that expression, he said it in Spanish—*cara de vinagre*, which literally means "face of vinegar." So *sourpuss* basically describes the same thing: a disgusted face. Francis continues, "An evangelizer must never look like someone who has just come back from a funeral! Let us recover and deepen our enthusiasm, that delightful and comforting joy of evangelizing" (10). So you see, it is simple: if you want to be a witness to Christ, choose joy, and don't be a sourpuss!

Throughout my school years, I did not excel academically, but I certainly excelled socially. Upon high school graduation, my classmates voted me "most popular" and "most rowdy." My parents were not impressed. During my first years of college, I remained much the same. But in my last year, I had a very real and powerful encounter with Christ. In my newfound fervor, I took myself and religious rules a bit too seriously—no more fun for this newly committed disciple. One day, after I ranted to my mom about what other so-called Christians should be doing, my mom, a devoted Catholic, said to me, "Where is my fun-loving daughter? I don't think God is asking you to give up your joy." Her words really shook me back to reality, and I realized my arrogance. God didn't need another sourpuss disciple. God instead invited me to follow with a new freedom—to become my best self and not turn into a plaster statue of someone else. I firmly believe joy, laughter, and compassion offer a much more compelling case for Christ than do rigidity and judgment. We are to witness with joy and through joy.

THE *Witness* OF *Scripture*

Rejoice in hope, be patient in suffering, persevere in prayer.
—Romans 12:12

When I think about joy, my two-year-old grandnephew, Braden, comes to mind. Braden's mom and dad, Courtney and Dan, ran with me in a 5K "Nun Run" sponsored by my Dominican congregation. As I was finishing the race, I spotted Braden jumping in and out of a puddle and laughing with glee. He was near the finish line, oblivious to the gasping runners as we approached our final goal. The steady drizzle, wet sneakers, and smudges of mud on his face did nothing to dampen his spirit or his enthusiasm for puddle jumping. Just watching him made me smile, and I couldn't help laughing along with him.

Many of the spectators, including some of my Dominican sisters, watched Braden, enjoying his playfulness. Even his mom enjoyed the moment, resisting the urge to clean him up and dress him in dry clothes. That day, Braden's playing in the puddle outside our convent chapel under the shadow of a huge statue of St. Dominic was a God-moment for me—a reminder that God's presence is revealed in the simple joys we all experience from time to time, if not each and every day. God is everywhere, and where God is, there is fullness of joy. Maybe a way to choose joy is to revive our desire to jump into puddles and resist the inner sourpuss that restrains us from letting go, playing, and delighting in life.

Joy is a gift from God, released in us by the power of the Holy Spirit. It does not depend on events, but on a deep belief that in God all will be well. We don't inherit joy, nor is it dependent entirely upon circumstances. Joy is woven into the life of the one who trusts and hopes in God. It remains accessible to us as a deep reserve of comfort and source of inspiration when life brings struggles or we lose our way. For followers of Christ, every action, event, and relationship in service of God and neighbor shares a joyful quality. The ongoing call to serve God and neighbor joyfully is the principle aim of our Christian life.

Even when times are rough, the Bible urges us to be joyful in hope. The verb *rejoice* appears seventy-four times, and the noun *joy*, fifty-nine times in the Christian scriptures. The psalms are full of references to joy. The psalmist leads the assembly in rejoicing in the truth that God is Creator and Redeemer of all. Because of God's covenant of unconditional love, the psalmist urges the assembly to "make a joyful noise to the LORD" (Ps 98:4).

When St. Paul speaks of joyful hope during affliction (see Romans 12:12), or urges the Philippians to "rejoice in the Lord always" (Phil 4:4), or names joy as a fruit of the Holy Spirit (see Galatians 5:22), the essential characteristics of Christian joy emerge. The joy of which our scriptures speak is focused on relationship with God in Christ. Mary sings of this joy in her Magnificat: "My soul magnifies the Lord, and my spirit rejoices in God my Savior" (Lk 1:46–47). The voice of Mary in the Magnificat (see Luke 1:46–55) is the voice of Christian faith revealing to those struggling alone that the power of God is with them as it was with her. She too was weak and alone, but when she welcomed the divine within her body, she was able to overcome adversity and sing with joy against the injustices of her day. We too can experience joy even during trials, while suffering, and in the face of demoralizing injustice. Witnessing to our faith and hope with joy, particularly during our own hard times, captures the hearts, minds, and hope of those with whom we share our stories. Followers of Jesus refuse to let happenstance or others' negative attitudes and unjust behaviors rob us of our joy. Instead, we face the truth of our situation and tackle it head on. Like Mary, we welcome the divine within us, giving us more than enough strength to confront the darkness that threatens us and our world.

I thank God for Braden, playing freely and joyfully witnessing to God's presence among us. I still need to be reminded not to take myself too seriously, and not to miss the way God reveals joy in my life every day. Sometimes I become so focused on the tasks I need to complete that I lose sight of the love that surrounds me and the many people and activities that bring me joy.

If our heads are down, and we are charging ahead with daily tasks, we may miss those surprise blessings that come our way—often when we need them most.

Seize the day, and take time to enjoy the people and activities that refresh your spirit. For all we have is now!

However old we are or whatever we are experiencing, St. Paul reminds us to "rejoice in hope, be patient in suffering, persevere in prayer" (Rom 12:12). Reach deep into your own joyful memories today to recall things that matter most in your life. Let those memories help you to step back, take a deep breath—or a few deep breaths—and choose joy, befitting a disciple of Christ Jesus.

THE *Everyday* *Witness* OF SR. *Mary* *Carmel* *McEneany*, O.P.

Sr. Mary Carmel McEneany was a member of my Dominican congregation and an everyday witness to joy. In her living, and most powerfully in her dying, she embodied Romans 12:12: "Rejoice in hope, be patient in suffering, persevere in prayer." When Sr. Carmel was diagnosed with terminal cancer at eighty-two years old, she was offered an aggressive treatment that promised a few additional months of life. She chose to transition from life here to life thereafter without treatment, to move peacefully and prayerfully into the arms of her God. Her journey to God was her finest teaching moment—witnessing to how to approach death with joy. As she embraced her death with prayer, patience, and peace, Sr. Carmel became a powerful witness to many of the sisters who lived with her at our motherhouse.

A few months before she died, I had a powerful visit with Sr. Carmel, just after Christmas. She radiated joy as she shared with me her anticipation of meeting God. I asked if she was afraid, and she just smiled as she told me that her whole life with God prepared her for the coming moment. She laughed as she shared with me about the pile of Christmas gifts she had received from her family. With a twinkle in her eye, she replied, "I will not need these where I am going." She recounted how she had told her sister, Barbara, also a Dominican sister, to pack up the gifts but to wait to use them or give them away until after Sr. Carmel had gone home to God, because she wanted to be sensitive to the gift givers. She instructed Barbara to leave the tags on the gifts, so people who received them would know the gifts were brand new. We laughed together. I had entered her room a bit anxious and sad, but I departed from her presence with renewed faith and a rediscovered joy. It was not what I expected.

For a quarter century, Sr. Carmel ministered at Dominican College in Orangeburg, New York. Known for her quiet smile and open door, Sr. Carmel inspired many students on their paths for life. She gave her life to others as a teacher, counselor, and administrator. In each of these ministries, her faith-filled witness and joyful spirit encouraged students to be their best selves.

In his book *Sacred Fire*, Fr. Ron Rolheiser, O.M.I., writes about the path to becoming a mature Christian. He describes midlife as a time of giving our lives away by striving to live for others instead of for ourselves. Sr. Carmel certainly did that. Then in the final stage of life, Rolheiser writes, there is a deeper call to Christ's disciples to give our deaths away. That is exactly what Sr. Carmel did. She gave an extraordinary gift to all those she left behind—she graciously, courageously, and joyfully gave her death away. Sr. Carmel's lifelong witness and joyful death magnified the Lord and inspired many to a renewed encounter with Christ.

Prompts FOR Self-Reflection

What person in your life radiates joy? Reflect on particular ways in which that person shows joy in their everyday life. How does that person bring *you* joy?

Recount a recent experience in which you witnessed joy.

Examine your life, and recall a recent time when you were a sourpuss and robbed another or yourself of joy. Write or offer in silence a brief prayer asking God for forgiveness and the courage to choose joy this and every day.

Growing THE Habit OF Joy

Ask: Pray every day this week for the grace of joy.

Be Aware: Think of someone who is joyful, and notice that person's smile or laugh.

Be Intentional: Choose a small behavior this week that will engender joy. Try smiling and laughing more.

Be an Everyday Witness: Share with someone a simple story of joy and how you experienced God in that experience.

Prayer TO Choose Joy

Good and gracious God,
I ask you for the grace to choose joy this day.
Free my spirit so I may smile at a stranger,
belly laugh with a friend,
and walk with a spring in my step.
Help me to see beyond my daily tasks
and make time for delight.
Strengthen me to resist my inner sourpuss,
which restrains me and stifles others.
May I be aware always that where you are, O God,
there is fullness of joy.
Give me courage to be a witness to joy this week

in my words and in my actions.
I ask this in the name of Jesus the Christ,
the joy of God.
Amen.

2.

BE HUMBLE

Begin WITH *Prayer*

For you have delivered my soul
    from death,
    and my feet from falling,
so that I may walk before God
    in the light of life.

—Psalm 56:13

Be

We must learn to be the persons God has created us to be, children of God. We are before God the jewels of his creation. Authentic humility is not about self-deprecation, but rather knowing who we are in relationship to our God. Being humble means having a healthy sense of our strengths and weaknesses; it means generously making our talents available for the common good. The first step to growing in humility is acknowledging that we walk upright in faith and are greatly blessed by our God. At the same time, we walk with the limp that comes from sin and human frailty. In both our blessedness and our frailty, our merciful God is present and always ready to pick us up and to set us back on the path of life. We pray like the psalmist: "O God, keep our feet from falling, so that we may walk before God in the light of life."

During an interview with Pope Francis, a Jesuit journalist asked, "Who is Jorge Mario Bergoglio?" "I am a sinner," the pope replied. People were both surprised and consoled by his answer. Yes, even the pope is a sinner. In a later interview published on December 2, 2015, in the Italian magazine *Credere*, Pope Francis said, "I am a sinner. . . . I am sure of this. I am a sinner whom the Lord looked upon with mercy. I am, as I said to detainees in Bolivia, a forgiven man. . . . I still make mistakes and commit sins, and I confess every fifteen or twenty days. And if I confess it is because I need to feel God's mercy is still upon me."

We can witness to God's mercy only if we have experienced mercy. If we don't sin, we don't need a savior. I believe a truly humble Christian is not a doormat but a powerful person who deeply believes that she or he is loved, wonderfully made, forgiven, and in possession of a myriad of God-given strengths. We depend upon God for everything and on all the goodness God has placed in our hearts. To be humble means to live freely, thanking God for all we have and for all our accomplishments, knowing all is gift. It also means that we approach another person with empathy and love instead of judgment.

THE *Witness* OF *Scripture*

What does the LORD require of you but to do justice, and to love kindness, and to walk humbly with your God?
—Micah 6:8

In this passage from scripture, the prophet Micah is clear on what God requires from the Israelites and from us—justice, kindness, and humility. Micah and the other prophets of the Old Testament continually proclaim that God requires inner conversion and a proper attitude of spirit: a humble disposition. Humility is a description of the heart's attitude toward God. The image of walking with God is one often used in the Bible. It is an image that moves us forward and invites us to continue becoming the persons God has called us to be—women and men who are wonderfully made. This ongoing process begins with us accepting our humanity—embracing our best or truest self and acknowledging our false self. St. Irenaeus, a second-century Church Father, noted that "the glory of God is a person fully alive." As Christ's witnesses we are most powerful when we are fully alive in God—when we allow God's grace to reveal our Godlike qualities of justice, kindness, and humility.

In our world the virtue of humility isn't always looked on as a positive. Humility is often associated with being passive, submissive, or insecure. Yet all through the scriptures, God calls us to be humble in mind and spirit. In Jesus' Sermon on the Mount, for example, Jesus teaches the eight Beatitudes, one of which upholds humility as a virtue that paves the way to a full life. Jesus says, "Blessed are the poor in spirit, for theirs is the kingdom of heaven" (Mt 5:3). In contrast to the world's view, then, one of the ways to live a happy and blessed life is to walk humbly with God—being proactive in serving others, taking moral leadership, and feeling secure in God's power within you.

Christian humility is not a weakness but a strength. It means to have neither your nose up in the air nor your shoulders slouched. It means not exalting yourself and not worrying about people's opinions of you. To walk humbly is to be not above someone or below someone, but rather *with* someone. It is not thinking you can do it all on your own and carrying the burdens of the world upon your limited human shoulders. Walking humbly with God is about using our God-given talents and not hiding them. It is about living with grace and not trying to play God. To walk humbly is to get up every day and thank God for the new day, restart without regret, and look into the mirror and say, "God loves me." With our hands clasped in the hand of our God, we move forward together on the path of life.

There is tale of a monk who was asked by a small boy, "What do you do all day in this monastery?" The monk replied, "Each day I walk, I stumble, I fall down, and I get up again and continue walking." There is something very freeing in this simple story. We all stumble and fall trying to walk in the footsteps of Christ. For me, the lesson is that I am human, and I often fall as I try to live as a follower of Christ. What a reality check! But the other side of that is an even more important truth: I am human, and I often do what is good and true and beautiful because, as the psalmist reminds me, "I am fearfully and wonderfully made" (Ps 139:14). By God's grace, mercy, and power, we walk on God's path of justice, kindness, and humility.

False humility can hurt us as much as false pride. We can use our feelings of inadequacy as an excuse for not becoming our best selves and using our gifts for the world. Each of us is a child of God and has been blessed—we are fearfully and wonderfully made. We are born to bring God's light to the world.

We are not born with feelings of inadequacy, think-ing that we are not enough. It is often life's negative expe-riences and emotions that create that sense within us. I attended a retreat in high school where one of the talks was titled "God Does Not Make Junk." After the talk, the retreat leaders gave us each a big yellow button with those words emblazoned on it. For a long time, I kept that button on my bedroom dresser.

We all need to internalize that message. Despite all the blessings in our lives, and our faith in God, we some-times can't shake that nagging feeling that we aren't good enough. Those old recordings in our heads kick in: "I should be a better person," "I should be more successful," "I am too fat, too thin, too *whatever*." And the negative talk goes on. These negative recordings do nothing to help us better ourselves but instead drain us of the pos-itive energy we need to do God's work—with what we have, with who we are, and at this moment in our lives.

Humility is love and justice in action, and true humility is free of arrogance and judgment. The heart of humility is captured in a common proverb based on 1 Corinthians 15:10: "There, but for the grace of God, go I." This proverb is a recognition that others' misfortunes, bad choices, or lack of faith could be ours, if it weren't for the grace of God.

Sharing our faith joyfully, gratefully, and with humil-ity is how we become powerful witnesses for Christ.

The prophet Micah speaks to us today: "What does the LORD require of you but to do justice, and to love kindness, and to walk humbly with your God?" (Mi 6:8). Are you willing to take on this challenge today?

THE *Everyday Witness* OF *Fr. Jim Conlan*

One of my heroes is Monsignor James S. Conlan, a priest who walked with a limp, known simply as Fr. Jim. He was a compassionate priest and powerful preacher who was just, kind, and walked humbly with his God. Fr. Jim was priest of the Archdiocese of New York, and he was the founder of the Archdiocese of New York's parish mission team. He preached through the power of story and was not afraid to reveal his vulnerability.

Fr. Jim lived his life with a withered leg as a result of polio. He wore an orthopedic shoe, and when he was tired, that leg dragged. There was no hiding this as his powerful upper body propelled him forward. By the time he entered my life, he was free from the burden of shame and bitterness over the effects of polio and was able to name it as a blessing. In my early twenties, before I entered the convent, I served as a member of the parish mission team, which became one of my most formative experiences in discipleship.

Fr. Jim was the heart of the team, and his preaching clearly demonstrated the power of witness to us and to packed churches. One of the stories he shared was how he gradually came to see the effects of polio not as a handicap but as a source of strength to testify to the Good News of Jesus Christ. He shared that he had a tough time playing sports while growing up because of his weakened leg. He was self-conscious and resented his lack of athletic prowess; he became a first baseman because it did not require much movement. One day, while Jim was walking to class at his Jesuit high school, an elderly Jesuit priest approached him and asked the dreaded question, "Son, did you have polio?" Jim shyly answered, "Yes." The priest asked, "You feel sorry for yourself, don't you?" and walked away.

At first, Fr. Jim explained, he was so angry, but as the priest's comment continued to haunt him, he began to acknowledge that there was some truth to the old Jesuit's words. Fr. Jim became aware of his anger and resentment and began the process of bringing it to God. He began to slowly realize that he could accept the effects of polio as a gift, rather than only a hardship, and that perhaps it might be the way to direct his life toward God. This realization gave him a deep empathy for people who suffered or had some disability.

This incredibly intelligent, deeply talented, and powerful preacher embraced the effects of polio as gift—a gift that empowered him to walk humbly with his God in service to the hurting. Like Jacob's limp described in Genesis 32:22–32, Fr. Jim's limp served as a reminder of his encounter with God. Like the "thorn in the flesh" that St. Paul endured (2 Cor 12:7), Fr. Jim's many and sometimes frightening falls served to keep this charismatic and much-loved priest humble and dependent on God. His limp also reminded him of the tremendous strength he did have that allowed him to overcome his physical and emotional impairments. It motivated him to develop a deep empathy and compassion for others, a hallmark of authentic humility.

On one day of a weeklong parish mission, we members of the team were rushing to get from a Mass upstairs to Mass in the lower church. Fr. Jim tripped at the top of a long flight of marble stairs and tumbled all the way down. When he hit the bottom, we heard a loud *thwack!*, and then came his puzzling words, "Thank you, Lord!"

This prayer was always on Fr. Jim's lips. No matter what happened, that was his response. In his experiences of thanking God for polio, of being rejected by the Jesuits because of his weakened leg, through every one of his five appointments as a priest, and of needing two liver transplants, this was always his prayer. I am fairly sure it was his last.

I learned many lessons from Fr. Jim about witnessing to our faith through humility, but two of the most important that I continue to practice are these: (1) before you speak, look out at the people and love them, and then you have the authority to speak; and (2) never be the hero or heroine of the story you share. When God works through one of our weakest moments, God's power and our hidden strengths are revealed in new ways. God is the hero of the story who gives us strength in our weakness. When we recognize this, it is then that we can empower others to discover God's presence in their own difficult situations.

Prompts FOR Self-Reflection

How is the world's definition of humility different from how we as Christians would describe it?

What person in your life exhibits humility? Reflect on ways that person shows humility and how it inspires and motivates you.

Examine your life, and recall a recent time when you failed or experienced weakness. How did God unleash a personal strength of which you were not fully aware?

Growing THE Habit OF Humility

Ask: Pray for the grace of humility.

Be Aware: Notice and claim a God-given strength in you.

Be Intentional: Reflect on a time when you lost your way or stumbled a bit. What was the strength that brought you back to God's path?

Be an Everyday Witness: Send a card to someone who is going through a difficult time. Let them know you are praying for them.

Prayer TO Be Humble

Good and gracious God,
I ask you for the grace of humility to know
that I am fearfully and wonderfully made.
Help me to accept the complex gift of being human:
my capacity for love and empathy
and my need for your forgiveness and healing.
Deliver me from arrogance, pride, and harsh judg-
    ment, and fill me with a sense of purpose.
Give me a new awareness of my strengths.
Lift me as I stumble, and set me on the right path.

No matter what happens, put the words "thank you"
     on my lips and gratitude in my heart.
Help me to be like Jesus, witnessing to your love and
     mercy with justice, kindness, and humility.
I ask this in the name of Jesus the Christ, our humble
     and merciful Savior.
Amen.

3.

PREACH FROM THE PULPIT OF LIFE

Begin WITH *Prayer*

O sing to the Lord a new song;
    sing to the Lord, all the earth.
Sing to the Lord, bless his name;
    tell of his salvation from day to day.
Declare his glory among the nations,
    his marvelous works among all the
    peoples.

—Psalm 96:1–3

Preach

Reading that we are all called to preach is likely a terrifying thing for many Catholics. Preaching belongs to priests and deacons and bishops, right? But preaching from the pulpit of life is a third habit to cultivate as an everyday witness to faith. We begin by praying with the psalmist, singing to God each morning. We thank God for the new day and for all of creation. We ask for the grace to notice the day-to-day sightings of God, and then we share them in simple and unobtrusive ways.

By "preaching from the pulpit of life," I mean two things. First, we ought to understand that our lives are our pulpits and that the way we live speaks loudly about God (or doesn't). Second, our lives become our pulpits to witness to our faith when we perceive God's activity in the world and share this knowledge with others each day. So preaching from the pulpit of life simply means to witness to our faith through the stuff of our lives. Unless our actions speak loudly of the God of love and justice, our words become, as St. Paul reminds us, "a noisy gong or a clanging cymbal" (1 Cor 13:1).

In my conversations, writings, and formal preaching as a member of the Order of Preachers (the Dominicans), I share my experiences of God from both my own life stories and those I have heard from others that deeply resonate with me. People ask me where I find all the stories, and the answer is simple: I look for them, note them, and sometimes write them down. I believe there are no coincidences in life, but only powerful moments when we can experience God working in ordinary ways. We discover these God-stories when we begin to reflect on life through a God-lens.

A few years ago, I realized my voice was getting hoarse. I thought it must be from all the talking I do—and my friends and family readily agreed! However, as the months went on, my voice grew hoarser; I finally decided to have my throat checked. I had a friendly conversation with a doctor, who told me it was probably caused by straining my voice. The doctor examined me by sticking a camera down my throat, and much to his surprise, and my shock, he discovered a lesion on my right vocal cord and suspected cancer. As with many of you, I felt overwhelmed by the C-word. I received a cacophony of advice from all interested parties. I embarked on an obsessive internet search; went for more tests, including two biopsies; sought a second opinion; and finally prepared for surgery.

There were many experiences of God's presence during that time, but one stands out. After surgery, I had to be completely silent for a week. For me, that alone required divine intervention. I decided it was best to spend the period of silence and recovery with my sister

Mary at her lake house in Upstate New York. As we were driving to her home, we experienced a downpour followed by a sudden clearing. There was an eerie silence between us. As we came around a sharp curve in the road, an exquisite full rainbow appeared before us. Mary spoke my immediate thoughts: "Look at the rainbow. It's a sign from God—all will be well." Wow! I experienced God's reassurance on a country road in Upstate New York. Mary pulled over, and I took a photo with my phone. I felt a new confidence that whatever the outcome of the surgery, God would be with me and give me the grace to deal with it. During my recovery, especially when I was feeling anxious, I reflected on that rainbow and once again experienced God's promise to accompany me. I like to share that story with others experiencing a health crisis and help them to locate in their own experience some reminder that God is with them too.

When we give witness to how God is working in and through our lives, we make God more comprehendible, more accessible, in a way—more real to others. As witnesses to the Gospel, we speak about God's marvelous works in the experience of our everyday world—in nature, in our work and in our leisure, and in our relationships with others. By the power of our baptism, we are sent forth to proclaim the saving love of our God and to tell of his faithfulness from day to day.

THE *Witness* OF *Scripture*

> But how are they to call on one in whom
> they have not believed? And how are they
> to believe in one of whom they have never
> heard? And how are they to hear without
> someone to proclaim him? And how are they
> to proclaim him unless they are sent? As it is
> written, "How beautiful are the feet of those
> who bring good news!"
> —Romans 10:14–15

I don't think I have ever heard anyone say to me or to
another, "Wow, you have beautiful feet!" Usually, it's the
opposite. When I played basketball in college, one season
I developed painful tendinitis in both feet. I went to a
podiatrist (one without a great bedside manner), and I'll
never forget what he said to me: "You have some wide
flippers—maybe you should forget basketball and join
the swim team." Occasionally, my two college room-
mates, Kay and Kathy, who accompanied me to that visit,
still tease me about my "beautiful flippers."

Feet are instruments of travel, and it is God's intent
for every Christian to walk on those beautiful feet and
go to those in need of God's healing word. St. Paul's message here to the community at Rome comes from Isaiah
52:7–8. Both Paul and the prophet Isaiah are calling their

communities to go out and be witnesses to the Good News of God's love. This doesn't mean you have to travel to remote parts of the world. People need healing everywhere. Both Isaiah and Paul walked through the countryside shouting out the message, wanting to reach as many people as possible, whether in one locale or in many. Paul made three long journeys on foot to visit many cities. Whether walking the hillsides, traveling through towns, or staying in one locale, Paul witnessed to the resurrected Christ and to what Jesus meant in Paul's life and for the world. We do not have to go to another town or country to bring the Good News, but we are sent to the people in our own communities—and to whomever our feet take us.

At age seventeen, my grandnephew Ben, an excellent student and standout athlete, was diagnosed with a rare form of cancer, which proved fatal. He left a legacy of courage after his year-long battle with the disease. More importantly, Ben embodied all that is good in the world and made all our lives better simply by sharing his life with us.

A few weeks before his last Christmas, I went to visit him and his family. They had recently received the devastating news that, despite aggressive treatment, Ben's chest cavity was filled with new tumors. He was six months into brutal and aggressive treatment for NUT midline carcinoma—cancer with no sure treatment plan nor cure.

Later, I sat in the hospital lounge talking with Ben's mom, my niece Tricia. She said to me, "Terry, Ben is my Jesus." She shared different ways in which Ben revealed God to her and told me a very memorable story about the way Ben chose to celebrate his eighteenth birthday, which they had recently celebrated. Unlike most kids his age, Ben fought hard to get to this milestone, and unlike most birthday celebrations, this one was in the oncology clinic at New York Presbyterian Hospital with no fanfare, no special dinner, and no friends.

Ben enjoyed making people feel good. He valued kindness and was known for making people feel like they mattered. During this entire experience, Ben made a lot of friends at the hospital—doctors, nurses, food handlers, and many others. He developed a special friendship with a young man named Michael who worked as a parking valet attendant at the entrance of the hospital. Michael and Ben bonded quickly—both were deeply kind and old souls. They were always so happy to see each other, catching up on sports, cracking jokes, and laughing. One day, Michael was going on about how well dressed Ben always was and how he had the coolest sneakers.

Ben had been very fast on the track and on the soccer field, and his beautiful feet were always clad in the best of sneakers. About a week before Ben's birthday, Tricia and Rob (Ben's dad) asked him what he wanted for his birthday. Ben replied, "I really want to get a pair of sneakers for Michael, the valet guy. I want to get Michael the same sneakers I have, but in black so he can wear them to work with his uniform." You can imagine the surprise and awe that Tricia and Rob felt hearing Ben's request. Tricia said, "We pulled up to the valet station a few days later with a wrapped box for Michael. Ben was so excited to give Michael the gift, simply saying, 'This is for you. Thanks for always being so nice to me.'" Later that day, Tricia told Michael that it was Ben's birthday. She told him what Ben had asked for, and Michael cried.

Reflecting on this last birthday, Tricia wrote, "We celebrated Ben's eighteenth birthday with our hearts, full of deep gratitude for the blessing of our son, for everything he brought to our lives, for the incredible impact he has made on us, for the many ways he has changed our lives for the better, and for what he has taught us about living. That was Ben's last birthday, but we will celebrate him forever—his life and his fight; his strength, grace, and humility; his unwavering loyalty, incredible kindness, and fierce sense of humor. We will celebrate Ben's powerful empathy, deep compassion, and effortless forgiveness each and every day, forever."

Ben preached from the pulpit of his life. Tricia preached from the pulpit of her life. Hearing Ben's birthday story lifted my spirit when I thought I was there to support and comfort Tricia. That day Ben became my Jesus too. "How beautiful are the feet of those who bring good news!" (Rom 10:15).

THE *Everyday Witness* OF *Bobby Williams*

Each of you know people who inspire you to be your best self—men and women who, as did Ben, bear the Good News by their generosity and kind acts, people who live the way of Jesus. Bobby Williams is also one of those people. On the surface, Bobby is a regular guy who built a very successful business, a good marriage, and goes to church on Sunday. He is engaging, funny, and at the same time humble. Bobby is also extraordinary in the way he lives his faith. He has answered Christ's call to witness to his faith by reaching out to the poor, the vulnerable, and the neglected. He reaches out beyond himself, his family, and his parish to help those in need, especially homeless youth.

Bobby was baptized in the Catholic Church and then raised in the Baptist tradition. He never had what we often refer to as "a personal encounter with Jesus," and as he grew into adulthood, he stopped going to church. He says that when he was in the military he felt disdain toward men who were religious. Bobby explained, "I thought they needed someone to support them for things they couldn't do themselves. I didn't respect that." It wasn't until Bobby met his wife, Carol, that things began to change.

Carol not only professed her faith but also lived that faith by reaching out to others. Bobby said, "It wasn't anything Carol said, but because of the way she lived her faith that I decided to go to Mass with her." One Sunday, Bobby heard the invitation to anyone who wanted to be a Catholic to come and join a small group to share faith and prepare for the sacraments. "So, I went that Tuesday, got involved in this small community, and I ended up going to the group from September all the way through the Easter Vigil Mass. During the Easter Vigil, I was confirmed in the Catholic Church," he recalls.

After Bobby was confirmed, he and Carol joined a small faith-sharing community at their parish. Later, Bobby joined a men's small community that not only helped him to share his faith but moved him to action— to live his faith. Bobby became more aware of the plight of the homeless, and he found that he could use his gifts and talents to help runaway youth. Bobby's coming to faith both through talking with others in his small groups and by helping others in great need has given a deeper meaning and purpose to his life. "Covenant House, the parish, and my small Christian community allow me to move into somebody else's world," he says. "When I do that, and I feel good about myself, I know that I'm connected to the Body of Christ."

Bobby is one of the leaders of a fundraiser for Covenant House New Jersey called the "Sleep Out." Volunteers raise money by getting sponsors to make a monetary pledge to them or their team for spending the night on the street as many vulnerable youth do every night. The volunteers spend the first part of the Sleep Out evening getting to know some of the young people whose lives will be made better by the event. Then, they sleep in cardboard boxes alongside the city streets. By sleeping in a box and sleeping bag on a cold night for the benefit of homeless youth, Bobby preaches from the pulpit of his life. How beautiful are the feet of those who bring Good News!

Prompts FOR Self-Reflection

Think of a person who inspires you by the way they live the way of Jesus. How is that person making a difference in the world? How do they reveal the goodness of God to you?

Do you hesitate to share God-moments with others? If so, what do you think causes your hesitation?

Have you ever jumped at the chance to share a God-story? If so, what was the outcome for you and for whoever heard your story? If not, can you identify an upcoming opportunity to do so?

Growing THE *Habit* OF *Preaching* FROM THE *Pulpit* OF *Life*

Ask: Pray for the twofold grace to live your faith and for the courage and wisdom to know when to share God-stories.

Be Aware: Note people who engage in charitable works or just actions because of their faith in Christ.

Be Intentional: Each night this week, write the name of someone who brought you Good News that day by their simple act of kindness to you or another.

Be an Everyday Witness: Share a story about someone who inspires you by the way they live their faith.

Prayer TO *Preach* FROM THE *Pulpit* OF *Life*

Good and gracious God,
help me to preach your goodness from the pulpit of
    my life.
Slow me down as I walk this day,
so I may be more attentive
to your presence and activity in my day.
Walk with me as I go to both ordinary and amazing
    places to share your love.
Open my heart to those in need, and give me the
    confidence to help them.
Give me the courage to share my God-moments
and to make my feet beautiful by bringing Good
    News to others.

I ask this in the name of Jesus the Christ,
and through the power of the Holy Spirit.
Amen.

4.

PRAY UNCEASINGLY

Begin WITH Prayer

Rejoice always, pray without ceasing,
give thanks in all circumstances; for
this is the will of God in Christ Jesus
for you.

—1 Thessalonians 5:16–18

Pray

A fourth habit of an everyday witness to faith is praying unceasingly. In the scripture passage here, Paul

advises the Christian community at Thessalonica to make joy, unceasing prayer, and gratitude part of their everyday lives. He wants them to be ready when Jesus Christ comes at the end of time or at the end of each life. The Christian commitments to continued prayer and a life of joy and thanksgiving have their source in deep gratitude for Christ's saving action in our lives. These Christian dispositions not only are God's will for our personal lives, but they also provide the spiritual resources and inner strength we need to be powerful witnesses to Christ through the practices of hospitality, encouragement, and explicit support of others. These others may be lax in their faith, fainthearted, despairing over some great loss, or anguished by the abuse and cover-up scandal plaguing our Church. We are to be witnesses to our faith as best we can to those who have lost their way, turned away from God, let go of relationship with Christ, or abandoned the Church for whatever reasons.

St. Monica is remembered for her unceasing prayer for the conversion of her son, Augustine of Hippo. Before Augustine became a renowned saint, he was a notorious sinner. Monica did not badger him with threats of hell or cutting him off from her love, but hoped and prayed that her son would find joy and fullness of life in Christ.

Augustine was gifted and brilliant, but struggled to find his way. He lived promiscuously and fathered a son outside of marriage. Monica refused to give up on

Augustine and continued to pray and fast daily that he would discover Christ. Monica developed a friendship with Ambrose, the bishop of Milan. Ambrose was one of the four original Doctors of the Church—known as both a holy man and a great Christian thinker. Monica introduced Augustine to Ambrose, and these two men began an ongoing dialogue about the meaning and purpose of life, the conditions of Italian society, and the tenets of the faith. Augustine eventually converted to Christianity and grew into one of the most influential thinkers in Western history.

Monica exemplifies a parent who prayed unceasingly for her son to encounter Christ and to change his lifestyle. She couldn't convince Augustine with words—whenever she tried to talk to him about religion, he brushed her away. When Monica complained to Ambrose that Augustine would not listen, he urged her, "Speak less to Augustine about God and more to God about Augustine." Through her daily prayerful intercession for more than fifteen years, Augustine came to Christ and the Church.

The story of St. Monica and of St. Augustine's eventual conversion teaches us that it often takes someone other than us to bring a loved one to Christ—for the first time or once again. If you are praying for someone you love to come back to church or to find Christ, pray that they will meet someone who will be a positive influence as Ambrose was for Augustine.

THE *Witness* OF *Scripture*

Then Jesus told them a parable about their need to pray always and not to lose heart. He said, "In a certain city there was a judge who neither feared God nor had respect for people. In that city there was a widow who kept coming to him and saying, 'Grant me justice against my opponent.' For a while he refused; but later he said to himself, 'Though I have no fear of God and no respect for anyone, yet because this widow keeps bothering me, I will grant her justice, so that she may not wear me out by continually coming.'" And the Lord said, "Listen to what the unjust judge says. And will not God grant justice to his chosen ones who cry to him day and night? Will he delay long in helping them? I tell you, he will quickly grant justice to them. And yet, when the Son of Man comes, will he find faith on earth?"
—Luke 18:1–8

At the time of Jesus, in what we now call the Middle East, a woman had little social, economic, or political power. She had little authority or control over her own affairs, and a woman without a husband was stripped of what little position and material goods she might have had when married. In the Gospel of Luke and in the Acts of the Apostles, a widow is frequently used as an image of powerlessness. The point of this passage is that if a poor widow who prayed persistently could change the mind of an unjust judge, how much more our gracious God will respond to one who prays persistently. This parable encourages constancy in prayer and reassures us that God hears us. Earnest petitioning fortifies resolve, gives rise to hope, and helps us cast ourselves humbly into the arms of God.

Many of us can relate both to the prayer of Monica for the conversion of her son and to the unrelenting prayer of the widow asking for justice. Prayer is a powerful tool to make God's reign a reality in our world. As St. Monica learned, often our words have less effect than our actions. When our conversation about God with a loved one deteriorates into arguments and harsh words, it's time to step back, take a deep breath, and talk to God about that person.

However, prayer does not take us off the hook. We are to pray for our family and friends who no longer profess or practice their faith, but we must also become the message of God's love and justice for them. The Fuller Youth Institute in California has done extensive research on what helps young people stick with faith into adulthood—what they call "sticky faith." One of their findings is that most children who returned to the faith of their family had faith-filled parents who were patient and supportive even when they left their faith. It seems that the best way to bring back your child to faith is to love them even more tangibly than before they left, and to pray daily for them.

As I mentioned earlier, before I became a sister I was a member of the Archdiocese of New York's parish mission team. One of my colleagues was Jaime Rickert. Jaime is a very talented musician, song writer, and performer. Jaime often shared his witness story on the second night of the mission, which had the theme "Our Response to God's Love." He shared the dramatic story of his conversion and talked about his reckless lifestyle abusing drugs and alcohol and spiraling through fleeting relationships. He had traveled the world as a performer until he hit a dead end, having pretty much abandoned his family and contacting his mother usually only when he needed money.

Jaime would tell the mission attendees, "My mom often tried to speak with me about her faith, and for much of my life I listened politely and let her words pass in one ear and out the other. But when I was considering ending my own life, I remembered the fifteen minutes I spent with my mom in an airport. We hadn't seen each other in a year. I was going to meet her for a brief reunion at La Guardia airport in New York between flights. On the flight, I spent most of the time preparing my responses for the things I was sure she would say: 'When are you coming home? Why are you wasting your life? Look what you're doing to yourself and your family!'"

When Jaime arrived, though, all his mother said was, "Hi, son! It's good to see you. How are you?" He wasn't prepared for that response. Years later, when Ada, his mother, was asked how she had been able to act that way, she replied: "God loves me exactly as I am; how could I love my son, Jaime, any less?" So, because of his mom's prayerful and loving example of God's love and her own witness to her faith, Jaime turned to the God who loves each of us exactly as we are. Faith is contagious—Jaime caught it from his mom.

Ada loved Jaime through it all and continually prayed for him. He was the prodigal son, living with reckless abandon, and his mom was the prodigal parent, loving him with reckless abandon. She never stopped praying for Jaime and supporting and loving him. Even the most religious parents and best parenting can't guarantee that children won't, at least for a time, walk away from the faith in which they were raised. Research does shows that loving them and waiting patiently for them is a determining factor in whether those children will return to God. I would also add that prayer is an important factor.

THE *Everyday Witness* OF *Ada Rickert*

Jaime recently retired from forty years of full-time ministry as a musician, song writer, and parish minister—witnessing to his faith through story and song. His mom, Ada, lived to see ninety-nine, a quiet and lovely woman with a huge heart and a fierce love for God and her son. I remember her well. I was so taken by her faithful witness and loving presence that I asked Jaime to share with me about his mom and how she was a humble and prayerful witness of faith to him and to so many others. He told me, "My mother could find four-leaf clovers anywhere. It was annoying. I would look in a patch of grass for twenty minutes with no result; then she would look in the same place and find one in like thirty seconds. Okay, maybe a minute. I suppose I was relying on my own abilities. She relied on faith."

Ada would say she caught her faith from her parents. They were simple, working-class Scots who moved to the United States around 1910. Their faith was solid, and their goodness contagious. On Sunday, the whole family went to the Dutch Reformed church for morning services; the children went back for Bible study; then they all went to the Episcopal church because they liked the choir; and finally, they finished the day at the Pentecostal revival because they all liked to sing.

They were also a family known for living their faith through charitable works. There were special signs that hobos would leave near houses where a good meal or a handout was available, and Ada's house was marked as one of these places. When Jaime's grandmother was in her nineties, Jamie asked her, "Do you still believe in God?" She said, "Yes! And when I go to sleep at night, I give my troubles to God and I sleep like a rock! That's it. God loves us—that's the whole thing."

When Ada met Jaime's father, she became a Catholic and raised Jaime in the Catholic Church, and she always continued her life of prayer. "Yes, my mom prayed constantly; her life was a prayer," Jamie said.

There was a woman who lived up the street from Ada, and like her, was a widow with one son who lived far away from home. Every Christmas, Easter, and Thanksgiving, Ada made a nice dinner and brought a plate, first to her sister who lived nearby, and then to the neighbor woman. Ada ate her meal with the woman and listened to her as she spoke of how badly the world had treated her (it hadn't), how thoughtless and uncaring her son was (he wasn't), and all the other perceived difficulties of her life. Jaime once asked his mom why she went. Ada said, "She's all alone; somebody has to do it." Ada was that "somebody." She didn't pat herself on the back for doing it, or for the many other things she did for those in need.

When she was in her seventies, Ada was asked to become a communion minister to the homebound. She declined, saying she did not think she was worthy; but Jaime encouraged her to accept, and in the end, she did. Ada brought her autoharp and added a bit of music to each visit with the homebound members of her parish community, creating great demand for her visits. Once again, Ada became that "somebody," that beautiful person sharing God's presence in her acts of kindness, her words, and her simple music as well as in Holy Communion.

At her ninetieth birthday party, Jaime proposed a toast to her as the person in his life who most lived these words often attributed to St. Francis: "Preach the Gospel at all times, and if necessary, use words." He added, "She didn't use words often, but, my goodness, did she preach!" Jaime recalled, "I never heard my mom say a harsh word either to or about anyone. She believed that God loved her exactly as she was, 'warts and all,' and, 'If

God loves me that way, how can I offer anything less?'"
She dedicated her life to passing that love along.

Jaime had asked his mom about the way she treated everyone. Her answer was short and simple: "It isn't always easy, but it is always worth it." Faith is contagious, and Jaime and so many others caught it from Ada, who never ceased to pray.

Prompts FOR Self-Reflection

Name a person who prays with persistence and hope. How have you been inspired by that person?

Recount a recent experience in which you witnessed an answer to prayer.

Think of a person who has lost faith, and reflect on the ways you love that person. Begin to pray for that person to find a way back to God. How can you be more tangibly patient and more loving to that person?

Growing THE Habit OF Praying Unceasingly

Ask: Pray for the grace of perseverance in prayer.

Be Aware: Reflect on the ways God has answered your prayers.

Be Intentional: Pray specifically for a person to come back to God and the Church.

Be an Everyday Witness: Be more tangibly patient and loving to a person who has left the Church.

Prayer TO Pray Unceasingly

God of mercy and everlasting love,

I pray for the grace to pray unceasingly with a heart filled with hope and faith.

Make joy, prayer, and gratitude part of every day.

Give me all the resources I need to practice hospitality and encouragement of others.

I lift up to you those who are seeking you and need healing.

Help me to be patient and understanding with my loved ones who no longer practice our faith.

I entrust [Name(s)] into your merciful arms.

I ask this in the name of Jesus, the power and compassion of God.
Amen.

5.

LISTEN WITH A CUPPED EAR

Begin WITH *Prayer*

Let me hear what God the LORD will
  speak,
    for he will speak peace to his people,
    to his faithful, to those who turn to
      him in their hearts.

—Psalm 85:8

Listen

Listening well, with a "cupped ear," is a fifth habit to develop as an everyday witness of faith. James Bullock, a communication scholar and a preacher, has written a book titled *Preaching with a Cupped Ear*. In the book, he describes a drawing of a wise man that hangs on the wall of a professor's study. The charcoal image is large and a bit blurry. Its borders are unclear and seem to run together, but after gazing at it for a while, one sees the image becomes clearer. It appears to be a portrait of a rabbi, with a long beard that flows into his robe. He is seated, as rabbis are when they teach, but rather than having his mouth open to speak, the rabbi has one hand cupped behind his ear. The first lesson the rabbi teaches us is to listen rather than to speak.

To be effective witnesses to Christ's redeeming love, we need to listen both to God and to those with whom we are moved to share our faith stories. We need to witness through deep listening—with a cupped ear rather than an open mouth. We pray with the psalmist that we may hear God's word of peace and turn to him with our hearts wide open. We ask for the grace to listen to our neighbor with a cupped ear and without judgment, so they too may turn to God and be filled with peace. There are, of course, many times in sharing Christ's love that listening is much more appropriate than speaking. I learned that lesson early in my ministerial life while working in a parish in the South Bronx.

A distraught young father named César came to the parish office asking for me. His wife had just been diagnosed with stage-four ovarian cancer, and he had two young boys to care for. The young family had recently immigrated to the United States from El Salvador to escape the perils of the civil war there. They were finally settled in and doing well—until the devastating diagnosis. I knew the mother and the two boys, but I had never met César.

César came into my office and sat across from me. He poured out his heart for an hour. At that time, I was just learning to speak Spanish. I got the gist of the story but few of the details. Occasionally, I said *si* (yes) or *esta bien* (okay). I felt so inadequate in trying to help this man. At the end of the conversation, I prayed a simple prayer with him in my broken Spanish. César began to cry and thanked me profusely for helping to ease his burden. All I had to offer was a compassionate heart, some simple Spanish words, and most importantly a cupped ear. The following Sunday, this man who rarely attended Mass was in the pew with his wife and boys.

There will be days when the most important witnessing we can do is to sit shoulder to shoulder with a hurting person, uncross our arms, lean forward, and hear their pain. In Dietrich Bonhoeffer's book *Life Together*, there is a section on the "ministry of listening." According to Bonhoeffer, there are many times when "listening can be a greater service than speaking." Good listening readies us to minister with words of grace to precisely the place where the other person is in need. As Bonhoeffer writes, "We should listen with the ears of God that we may speak the Word of God."

THE *Witness* OF *Scripture*

> You must understand this, my beloved: let every person be quick to listen, slow to speak, slow to anger.
> —James 1:19

This verse invites us to be better listeners to God and our neighbor. It is easy to understand, but it is hard to live.

I am very extroverted, and I must work hard at listening. I am also the fifth of six children in a strong and vocal family. Growing up in our family meant that if you wanted to speak, you usually just had to force your way into a conversation. Too often, I am slow to hear and quick to speak.

Good listening requires concentration, which means we need to have both ears cupped. It requires patience and a commitment to hear the other person until they are finished speaking. Rarely will a speaker begin with what is most important—it takes time and trust to speak our deepest thoughts and feelings. As a person who is quick to speak, I know only too well that it takes Spirit-powered patience not only to be quick to hear but also to keep on hearing.

My brother Joe is also a high extrovert, and I think he talks more than I do, but interestingly, he is easy to talk with and very inclusive. When he is aware, he can bring out the quietest person in the room and really listen to them. He told me that his New Year's resolution is to listen more. To remind himself of this, he put this message on his cell phone: "Note to self: keep your mouth closed and listen." We are each a work in progress, including my brother Joe, and although I would never say this to him, I think he is evolving.

Good listening means silencing the smartphone and not interrupting someone's story. It means being attentive to the present moment and to the person with whom we are shoulder to shoulder. It takes energy to block out the distractions that stream into our consciousness and to silence the voice inside that wants to interrupt with advice or to prompt someone to get to the point.

We live in a fast-paced culture where multitasking is not optional. Most children grow up with both parents working outside the home, and time together is a precious commodity—there is not much time to listen with a cupped ear. Even still, children need an adult to listen to them. When we listen to children, we show them we care, and when they know someone loves them, they are open to knowing the love of God.

I learned through my ministry with Latino families in the South Bronx the important role of the *abuela* (grandmother) in raising children and passing on the faith. One afternoon, I was helping prepare a group of seventh and eighth graders for the sacrament of Confirmation. Most of them were slumped in their chairs with disinterest and boredom. If I had been Jesus Christ or Mary, the Mother of God, maybe then they would have paid attention. I was teaching about the Trinity and introduced God as a loving Father. One of the boys sat up straight, raised his hand, and said, "Sister, if God is like my father, I don't want anything to do with him." Then they all began to talk about their experiences with their fathers, and it was probably the best theological reflection I ever had about images of God. So I said to them—it must have been the Holy Spirit—"Who in your life reflects a God who is loving and caring?" And they said almost in unison, "*Mi abuela*" ("My grandmother"). So, we began to explore God as *Abuela* and how that image could help them understand the nature of God. They talked about their *abuelas* loving and caring for them, always being there to listen, cooking and making sure there was plenty of food on their plates, making *sopa de gallinas* (chicken soup), slathering their chests with ointment when they had a chest cold, and praying over them as they were tucked in at night. They taught me a great lesson that day: how *abuelas*—women with big hearts and cupped ears—are beautiful images of God.

THE *Everyday Witness* OF *Evelyn Villalba*

In the Sacred Heart parish community of the South Bronx, I was graced with meeting and adopting an *abuela*. She was Evelyn Villalba, a leader in the parish who took me under her wing. When the pastor, a curmudgeonly and aging Irishman, hired me, he told me to meet with Evelyn, who would show me the ropes. It was the best pastoral advice he ever gave me.

Evelyn was born in Puerto Rico and came to the United States as a young child. Her parents died young, and she was adopted by her aunt, so her cousins became her sisters. She married later in life and never had children, both of which made her unusual in my new neighborhood. Evelyn had a chronic illness most of her life, but it never stopped her from being an active part of the religious, social, and charitable activities of the parish and neighborhood. She garnered respect from all in the barrio. She was always ready to listen and had buckets of love to share.

I often visited Evelyn in her small apartment. There I shared my wonderings and struggles as I tried to become an effective minister in a culture not my own and with a language I struggled to master. She always welcomed me, fed me, and listened attentively as I rambled on. As I ate her *arroz con habichuelas* (rice and beans), I would pour out my heart to her. Often, I would come with a talk I needed her to translate, and she would listen patiently as I practiced my Spanish. She corrected me and never let me off the hook. She wanted my Spanish to be perfect—and I appreciated her strong critique. She made sure what I said was not only clear but also culturally sensitive and meaningful to my listeners. She was one of my co-ministers in the parish RCIA program and became godmother and sponsor to many who joined the Church.

I spent eight wonderful years in that parish. I learned how to minister to and deeply love the people entrusted to me by God. I was formed and reformed during those years in that multicultural, immigrant, struggling neighborhood. When my Dominican congregation asked me to become formation director, I knew it was time to go, but I was so sad about leaving. The first person in the parish with whom I shared my leaving was Evelyn. I was not sure how she would take it. As we sat at her kitchen table, I poured out my heart. She sat with me shoulder to shoulder, leaned forward, and listened attentively to my ambiguity and pain. When I finished, she looked at me with a tear in her eye and said, "I am grateful that God brought you here, and now God has another plan for you. Don't look back, but bring us with you to your next ministry." I often returned to visit her, finding her with her Bible and rosary beads next to her easy chair. No matter how sick she became, she would always want to know what I was doing and how she could help. During one of my visits with her, she told me I was like her own. I simply said, "I am your own." I was privileged to speak at her funeral Mass. She may have had few blood relatives, but the church was filled with her adopted children, and I was honored to be one of them.

Evelyn had an open heart to embrace, a cupped ear to lend, and warm food to share—she was for me a great image of and witness to our everyday God.

Prompts FOR Self-Reflection

Who listens to you with a cupped ear? What has that relationship meant to you?

How can you improve your listening skills?

Growing THE *Habit* OF *Listening* WITH A *Cupped Ear*

Ask: Pray for the grace of listening with a cupped ear.

Be Aware: Be aware of times when you are listening well and times when you interrupt others. Stop thinking about what you want to say next and just be silent, so you can truly hear what the other person is trying to communicate to you.

Be Intentional: Jot down one action you can take to improve your listening skills.

Be an Everyday Witness: Give a call to someone who needs a "cupped ear."

Prayer TO *Listen* WITH A *Cupped Ear*

O God of open heart and cupped ear,
fill me with the gift of listening to you and to those
    entrusted to my care.
Help me to listen attentively so that I may speak your
    Word.

Come to my aid so I may be quick to hear and slow
　　to anger, and renew my desire to share my faith
　　with generosity and love.
May I hear your word with untroubled attention
so that I may share your love with those I meet today.
I ask this in the name of Jesus, the Word made flesh
　　who dwells among us.
Amen.

6.

PRACTICE THE ART OF ACCOMPANIMENT

Begin WITH *Prayer*

Do not fear, for I have redeemed you;
  I have called you by name, you are
    mine.
When you pass through the waters, I
    will be with you;
  and through the rivers, they shall not
    overwhelm you;
when you walk through fire you shall
    not be burned,
  and the flame shall not consume you.
                    —Isaiah 43:1b–2

Practice

One definition of the word practice is to "do something as a custom." So practicing the art of accompaniment simply means to grow accustomed to walking with others along their journeys of life. Sometimes that will mean keeping a friend company through an explicit questioning of one's faith, but often it simply means be a steady, trustworthy friend in everyday life. We recall God's own accompaniment of his people in this popular passage from the third book of Isaiah, which was written during a time when the Israelites were in exile and suffering under a foreign ruler. They were discouraged, shaken, and destitute. They needed to be reminded that God was with them and would accompany them during their time of crisis. They needed their faith bolstered and sustained by the prophets of their day—people who accompanied them and shared God's message of hope. I often need to hear the words: "Do not fear . . . I have called you by name, you are mine" (43:1). I take comfort that no matter what I am dealing with in my life, God is with me. I will not be overwhelmed. My worries, fears, and grief will not consume me.

Learning the art of accompaniment requires that we take our cue from the God who promises to be always with us, protecting and restoring us. The Bible presents a variety of ways in which God has graciously initiated a relationship with us fragile human beings and encourages and accompanies us in the everyday. The biblical God is presented as taking walks in the Garden of Eden with the first human beings; conversing with the prophets; and sending us Jesus Christ as God's unique Word among us and the Holy Spirit, our advocate, who continues to speak God's word today. The subject matter of God's ongoing conversation with us is an invitation to love and be loved—to know that we belong to God, who promises to be with us. Pope Benedict XVI taught us in his encyclical *Deus Caritas Est* (*God Is Love*):

> God is visible in a number of ways. In the love story recounted by the Bible, he comes toward us, he seeks to win our hearts, all the way to the Last Supper, to the piercing of his heart on the Cross, to his appearance after the Resurrection and to the great deeds by which, through the activity of the Apostles, he guided the nascent Church along its path. Nor has the Lord been absent from subsequent Church history; he encounters us ever anew, in the men and women who reflect his presence, in his word, in the sacraments, and especially in the Eucharist. (*Deus Caritas Est*, 17)

This God who loves us personally and guides us is made visible through the people who accompany us along our path.

Throughout my life, God has sent a variety of people to accompany me, at just the right time and place. These women and men have helped me to encounter Christ anew and deepen my faith, often during difficult times. Some are still part of my life, while others are not; but for each of them I am grateful. In turn, I have tried to answer the call to accompany others on their journey— sometimes for a day; maybe for a week, a few months, or several years; or perhaps for a lifetime. Those you accompany may include a friend, family member, or neighbor who is grieving or combatting a serious illness; a child in your religious education class; someone who chose you as godparent or sponsor for Confirmation; a friend who no longer attends Mass; or a person who is simply seeking a richer spiritual life.

There are five ways we can practice the art of accompaniment:

- Caring
- Listening
- Accepting
- Practicing patience
- Meeting people where they are

Being caring is the starting point. Remember, it is all about the little things when we're witnessing to the care and the love of God for another person. For example, someone who companions another encourages that person by pointing out all that is good in him or her and, by acts of kindness and generosity, helps that person come to personally know God's love and tender care for them. The most important gift we can give someone is our time, presence, and focused attention.

A second way to practice the art of accompaniment is to listen. Remember the cupped ear? Only through respectful and compassionate listening can we help another to discover what is already in their heart—God's love and purpose for their life.

A third way to accompany others is to accept them and not to judge them. Each person's situation before God and their life history is not fully known by us—and, sometimes, not even fully known or understood by that person.

A fourth way to live the art of accompaniment is to practice patience with others. The process of awakening and deepening faith proceeds slowly and does not follow a straight line. Transformation and healing don't happen in a single day or on a schedule. Sometimes we make great strides forward and then we have setbacks. The good news is that through God's mercy and grace, we can always reset and restart on our path toward God. We should keep this in mind for both ourselves and those we accompany.

A fifth, and possibly the most important, way to accompany people is to meet them where they are. We are focused on sharing our experiences of God. We want to share our faith, and we feel a desire to give to others what we ourselves have received. However, it's best to meet people where they are, so how and when we share our experiences of faith depends on the person and the situation.

My friend Cathy is a busy grandmother who accompanies her grandchildren on their journey to God and meets them where they are. She has five grandchildren ranging in age from three to ten years old. She races around running "Grandma's shuttle"—picking up kids at home and dropping them off at school, ball games, ballet, or wherever they need to be. She babysits several days a week and still manages to squeeze in attending games, recitals, and parties. Cathy always makes time for her family, friends, and most importantly her faith. One time when I was visiting her, she gave me a devotional book that included a bookmark with a picture of Our Lady. As I was leaving, the bookmark fell on the floor. Cathy's four-year-old granddaughter raced to pick it up and asked me if she could keep it. I told her, "Of course," but I asked, "Why do you want this bookmark?" Cathy's granddaughter said, "Because it has a picture of Mother

Mary." I was stunned that a four-year-old already knew of Our Lady.

Later, I asked Cathy how she connects the kids to their faith. She explained that she works hard to find ways to teach her grandchildren about God by meeting them where they are. She told me that her oldest grandson watches college football and roots for Clemson University. He also enjoys YouTube. Cathy searched YouTube and found a video of the Clemson quarterback, Trevor Lawrence, talking about his faith in Jesus Christ. She handed her grandson her cell phone and said, "Check out what your favorite Clemson quarterback said after the game."

Her grandson listened attentively as Trevor confidently witnessed to his faith in Christ. This big star said that while football was important, the most important thing in his life was his Christian faith.

Cathy has a deep desire to pass on the Catholic faith to her grandchildren—a faith that has made all the difference in her life. She accompanies her grandchildren on their faith journey by her care, listening to their troubles, accepting their imperfections, treating them with patience, and meeting them where they are by finding creative and fun ways to connect them with the wide Catholic tradition.

THE *Witness* OF *Scripture*

Now on that same day two of them were going to a village called Emmaus, about seven miles from Jerusalem, and talking with each other about all these things that had happened. While they were talking and discussing, Jesus himself came near and went with them, but their eyes were kept from recognizing him. . . .

As they came near the village to which they were going, he walked ahead as if he were going on. But they urged him strongly, saying, "Stay with us, because it is almost evening and the day is now nearly over." So he went in to stay with them. When he was at the table with them, he took bread, blessed and broke it, and gave it to them. Then their eyes were opened, and they recognized him; and he vanished from their sight.

—Luke 24:13–16, 28–31

The story of the presence of the risen Jesus on the road to Emmaus is the most powerful of the postresurrection appearance stories. Its plot revolves around the failure of the two disciples to recognize the "stranger" who accompanied them on their journey. As they walked, mired in grief and disappointment, they were in deep conversation about the things that happened to Jesus of Nazareth, the one they had believed was the Messiah. Jesus caught up with them, initiated a conversation, and asked what they were talking about. His question stopped them in their tracks. They were surprised that this man was unaware of all that had transpired over the last few days. First, Jesus listened. Then, he slowly revealed himself to them through the scriptures and, finally, in the breaking of the bread. As soon as they recognized him, he vanished.

Often, we have similar God-moments—fleeting religious experiences—but recognize or acknowledge them only in retrospect. This was an exceptional moment for these two disciples, one they then shared with the rest of the believers and anyone else who would listen.

The Emmaus story has a message for those of us who become disappointed and disheartened and feel the absence of God: Christ is always walking alongside each of us, just as he did with the disciples on the way to Emmaus. By faithfully reflecting on scripture and being nourished by the Eucharist, we truly come to recognize Christ's presence over and over again in our everyday journey. God also sends people into our lives, fellow travelers—sometimes friends and other times strangers—to accompany us during the most difficult and painful times of our lives.

In chapter 3, "Preach from the Pulpit of Life," I shared a story about my grandnephew Ben during his battle with cancer, when he gave the hospital parking valet, Michael, a pair of sneakers. During Ben's illness, he and his whole family were accompanied by a myriad of people: the hospital staff, school and parish communities, local townspeople, and business colleagues—some family, some friends, and some strangers. All these people rallied around Ben and his family.

Ben's mom, Tricia, is Catholic, while his dad, Rob, did not identify with any church at the time. Rob was fine with Tricia bringing their children up Catholic and attended Mass with his family on Christmas, Easter, and other special occasions. Rob shared with me that he wasn't anti-God or opposed to religion, but he just did not think much about God. After Ben's diagnosis, Rob felt drawn to attend early morning daily Mass. The daily routine, the peace of the church environment, and the prayers and scripture readings brought him strength and comfort.

To prepare Ben's funeral liturgies, Rob, Tricia, and I met with Fr. Stephen, the pastor of their parish. I will never forget Rob's parting words to Fr. Stephen: "Father, as you know I have been attending daily Mass. My dad was Catholic and my mom Presbyterian, and somehow, I was baptized Lutheran—I am all mixed up. After all the services are done, do you think you can help me straighten this all out?" We all chuckled, and Fr. Stephen immediately said, "Sure, Rob, happy to." Fr. Stephen began meeting with Rob, and he was received into the Church, made his First Communion, and was confirmed during the Easter season.

Rob shared with me why he became a Catholic, "When my life was going well, I didn't think much about God. But when Ben became ill and eventually died, it turned my life upside down." Rob began asking the big questions of life. He found consolation in God and his parish community, who supported him and his family through Ben's illness, death, and the aftermath. Fr. Stephen and many others accompanied Rob on his pilgrimage to God. In Rob's pain and disillusionment, Jesus made himself known through Rob's supportive parish community, in the Word, and most especially in the breaking of the bread.

THE *Everyday Witness* OF *Barbara Miller*

My friend Barb, whom I met through RENEW, is a powerful example of someone who accompanies others to Christ. She was as serious as she was funny. She was energetic, generous, and filled with purpose. No challenge seemed too great to her, and if anyone needed help, she was there. Most importantly, Barb reflected Christ, and she accompanied many on their pilgrimage to God. Barb walked away from the Church for a while but returned with renewed fervor for God and the Church. I think her experience of leaving the Church helped her to better understand and accompany others who had been disaffected by the Church for whatever reason.

Barbara grew up in a large Italian family. Her aunt and grandmother were very religious. With these strong role models, Barb witnessed what she called "a real love for and commitment to the Catholic Church." It was through the accompaniment of her family that Barb recognized she had a God-given gift for teaching, which led to her first teaching job in a Catholic school. She told me that she loved the kids but was disillusioned by the behavior of two priests at the school, and she began to distance herself from the Church. The last straw was when she offered her professional services as a pro bono counselor to her parish, but the pastor said, "No, thanks." Barb said, "So I just walked away." She continued, "I always identified as a Catholic and looked for a way to get back in touch with the Catholic Church."

Barb eventually found her way back to the Church through an invitation to join a RENEW small faith-sharing group in her local parish. The group accompanied her back into the faith. She returned with great zeal and threw herself into parish ministries and activities. After Barb retired from teaching, she became the director of faith formation in her parish. She expanded the parish's small-group ministry and began to offer retreats and conference days. I was a speaker at a couple of these events and I was always impressed on how organized they were and even more so by the numbers who attended. Barb ministered formally in the parish and informally to everyone she met. She did what Pope Francis urges each one of us to do, "to bring Christ from the sacristy and into the street." A few years after beginning her work as director of faith formation, Barb—so full of vim and vigor—was diagnosed with amyotrophic lateral sclerosis (ALS, also known as Lou Gehrig's disease).

During the many months of slow decline and suffering, she continued to witness to her tremendous faith. One day when I was visiting, I met her neighbor Rosemary, who told me how much Barb had helped her in her spiritual life. Their friendship started with a mutual desire to get in shape, so they started walking together. Rosemary said, "After walking together for many months, we 'crazy old ladies' decided to do a fitness boot camp." This experience of sweat and pain solidified their friendship, and their conversations began to deepen. Rosemary recalled, "Barb never forced her faith on me, but was always willing to listen. I began talking to her about my divorce, and then how I had turned away from God and the Catholic Church." She continued, "I knew Barb's faith ran deep, and it would have been easy for her to just say, 'You need to go back to church.' But she didn't do that. She never judged me. She just continued to patiently listen."

Over time Barb slowly accompanied Rosemary on her journey back to the Church. Rosemary recounted, "She shared books with me, invited me to church events, and suggested I visit different parishes. She encouraged me to return to Mass, offering to go with me. She even bought me a Sunday missal and showed me how to use it."

Barb also encouraged Rosemary to openly share her faith. Rosemary said, "Then, at just the right moment, she did something that at first was scary to me but has turned out to be a real blessing. She suggested I lead a RENEW faith-sharing group in my home. I felt so ill-prepared with little real 'Catholic' knowledge." Rosemary's small group has been together for more than six years. They meet faithfully for six weeks every fall and spring in Rosemary's home. She said, "I have expanded my knowledge of my faith. My experience with being part of the Church has been very rewarding; I've made new friends, and I've had the opportunity to share prayer and experiences of God. . . . Through my whole journey back to God and the Church, I knew Barb was next door praying for me to stick with my journey . . . accompanying me all along the way."

Rosemary remembered, "In Barb's last months, I had the pleasure of taking her daily to morning Mass. Seeing her strong faith never wavering throughout her illness continues to keep me focused on my faith. I know she still accompanies me now, from above instead of next door. Karen, Barb's best friend, gave me a frame, and I put Barb's picture in it. It is at my bedside. I look at her photo every morning and night. She's with me, still. Sometimes you don't immediately realize the impact a person has on you or how they accompanied you." Rosemary concluded her reflections with these words: "All I can say is thanks, Barbara Miller!"

Barb's accompaniment of Rosemary was a powerful expression of faith and love that changed both women's lives.

Prompts FOR Self-Reflection

How did Barb reflect the five ways of accompaniment
explored above?

Who has accompanied you on your faith journey? How
did they accompany you?

Reflect on how Cathy reached out to her grandson. How might you use social media or another creative way to reach out to a young person in your life?

Growing THE *Art* OF *Accompaniment*

Ask: Pray for the grace to accompany a person on their journey to God.

Be Aware: Reflect on the ways you influence others in the faith.

Be Intentional: Invite someone to go to Mass with you or to another spiritual event.

Be an Everyday Witness: Accompany someone who is struggling by performing an act of kindness for them.

Prayer TO Practice
THE Art OF Accompaniment

Companion God,
as I walk down the journey of life,
thank you for sending your son, Jesus,
to accompany me.
Just as he was present to the disciples of Emmaus
and their eyes were opened, I know he is present on
    my journey with all its ups and downs.
I know him most intimately in the Word and
    Sacrament.
Thank you for the people you bring into my life
to accompany me on my pilgrimage of faith—
family, friends, and strangers
who walk with me as I grow in faith
and in my desire to be an everyday witness to you,
    O Lord.
Give me the generosity, confidence, and gifts I need
to accompany others on their journey
toward a deeper relationship with you.

I ask this through Jesus, my constant companion,
and by the power of the Holy Spirit.
Amen.

7.

ENGAGE IN GOD-TALK

Begin WITH *Prayer*

Blessed be the name of the LORD
   from this time on and forevermore.
From the rising of the sun to its setting
   the name of the LORD is to be praised.
   —Psalm 113:2–3

Engage

Engaging in God-talk is our final rallying cry in this book. Like the psalmist in the above opening prayer, we should bless and praise the Lord every day—from sunrise to sunset. We bless God's name by giving thanks, acknowledging God's presence, and treating God's name as holy. I believe God's name is blessed when we bring God into our everyday—when we engage in spiritual conversations or God-talk. This is the seventh and final habit to develop as we become more effective in our everyday witnessing to our faith.

In our culture, "God-talk" often means a general emotional outburst when something shocking has been discovered: we hear, "Oh, my God!" God's name is also mindlessly used to curse a person or a situation. Often, God's name is used in vain for as little as a golf ball hit into a bunker or a missed putt (as an admitted "golf nut," I know how frustrating these situations can be). Sometimes we do this same thing in a positive way, such as when someone recovers from a grave illness, and we say, "Thank God!" Or in a more trivial way, we might say, "Thank God, I got ahead of the traffic." The point is, whether good or bad, there is not much thought about God in this God-talk—just mindless figures of speech. In our increasingly secular society, I fear even these banal references to God will eventually phase out.

In a *New York Times* op-ed essay (from October 18, 2018) titled "It's Getting Harder to Talk About God," Jonathan Merritt highlights the lack of spiritual or religious conversations among more than three-quarters of Americans. Merritt cites a survey he conducted with Barna Group, a social research firm focused on religion and public life, which found that only 13 percent of Christians who regularly attend church had a spiritual conversation once a week. My hunch is that it would be even less for Catholic Christians. Merritt went on to cite several reasons why Americans shy away from discussions about God or their faith. He writes, "According to my survey, a range of internal conflicts is driving Americans from God-talk. Some said these types of conversations create tension or arguments (28 percent); others feel put off by how religion has been politicized (17 percent); still others report not wanting to appear religious (7 percent), sound weird (6 percent) or seem extremist (5 percent). Whatever the reason, for most of us in this majority-Christian nation, our conversations almost never address the spirituality we claim is important." Merritt warns that when Christians fail to talk about their faith, they allow people like "prosperity preachers" and politicians the space to control the narrative on Christianity—people who often use the Gospel for financial gain or to promote their unjust agenda. Our lack of sacred speech allows the worst among us to define Christianity for the masses.

Another interesting point in the article is the data describing the decline in the use of terms associated with moral virtue, which we Christians recognize as fruits of the Holy Spirt (see Galatians 5:22–23)—words such as *love, patience, gentleness,* and *faithfulness.* Even gratitude words such as *thankfulness* have declined. Merritt points out, "When you combine the data about the decline in religious rhetoric with an emerging body of research that reveals how much our linguistic landscape both reflects and affects our views, it provides ample cause for alarm."

As much as I believe that increasing our God-talk is important, I also know it can easily turn people off. So here are some of my "dos and don'ts" for God-talk.

Do try to use virtue words in your everyday conversations—words such as *love, gratitude,* and *kindness.* I belong to a fitness program called the "MAX Challenge," which combines fitness classes, nutritional counseling, and motivation. After each fitness session we have a couple of minutes of motivational talk. One day the trainer asked what blocks us from reaching our goals—from being our best selves. One woman shouted out, "I need a chef!" Another responded, "I love chocolate"—we all laughed. Then another called out, "I need forgiveness." It stopped the trainer in his tracks, and an unusual and uncomfortable silence followed. The woman explained, "I gained back some of the weight that I lost and just can't forgive myself. So, I just keep eating things that are bad for me." What followed was a sacred conversation about the power of forgiveness and about treating ourselves and others with compassion. As I was changing into my street shoes, one of the women from my class sat beside me and began talking to me about faith and forgiveness. God-talk on the exercise mats—I was happy to engage.

Do talk about what your faith means to you, do say what you are grateful for, and do share about the power of prayer. Do offer prayers for someone in need, whatever their religious affiliation, if any. I have had Jewish people, people from other Christian communities, and those with no religious affiliation ask me for prayers. I admit that because I am a nun, people feel free to ask me for prayer, but I find that friends who are public about their faith are also frequently asked for prayers. My coworker Susan shared this story with me. She said, "When my mother worked in a ladies' dress shop in Westfield, she was the only Catholic sales person—most of the women were Jewish. Whenever someone couldn't find something, they'd say, 'Dot, can you say a prayer to that saint of yours?' My mom would remark, 'St. Anthony always comes through!'"

Do tell people why you go to church and why is it important to you. Do comment on how you experience God in a beautiful sunrise or in other natural events.

Don't tell people what they should do and believe. Don't speak in a pious, superior tone when talking about things of God. Don't start with doctrine unless someone initiates that with a question. Don't tell someone to go to church; instead, tell them why you go. Share how hearing God's Word and receiving the Eucharist in community enriches your life.

THE *Witness* OF *Scripture*

Hear, O Israel: The LORD is our God, the LORD alone. You shall love the LORD your God with all your heart, and with all your soul, and with all your might. Keep these words that I am commanding you today in your heart. Recite them to your children and talk about them when you are at home and when you are away, when you lie down and when you rise. Bind them as a sign on your hand, fix them as an emblem on your fore-head, and write them on the doorposts of your house and on your gates.
—Deuteronomy 6:4–9

In this passage from Deuteronomy, we find the heart of the Jewish faith: a profession of absolute love for God, the importance of talking about things of God in the everyday, and the instruction to pass on the love of God to children.

The Shema (see Deuteronomy 6:4–5, 11:13–21; Numbers 15:37–41) became the principal profession of Jewish faith. At the time of Jesus, it was so influential that Jesus used it as the beginning of his answer to the question about the greatest commandment. A scribe asked Jesus, "Which commandment is the first of all?" Jesus replied, "The first is, 'Hear, O Israel: the Lord our God, the Lord is one; you shall love the Lord your God with all your heart, and with all your soul, and with all your mind, and with all your strength'" (Mk 12:28–30). Even today, the Shema is the first prayer Jewish parents teach their children.

According to Deuteronomy, the people are instructed to engage in conversation about the love of God when they are at home and on the road. These words must be actively taught to children. This reading and others gave rise to two Jewish practices. The first practice is wearing small leather boxes called *phylacteries,* containing verses from this scripture passage. The other practice is placing a small decorative case called a *mezuzah,* containing a scroll with the Shema on it, on the doorpost of the home. Devout Jews touch it when they go into the house and when they leave. I love that practice of taking the Word with you not only into the family space but out into the world. The point is to bring the Word of God from the synagogue to the home, and then with you as you go about your daily activities.

We too are called to bring the Word of God into our homes and to talk about God with our children. Therefore, we put a cross on the wall in our bedrooms and other religious symbols in our homes. Prayer at meal times is an especially important way to bring God-talk into our families and households. I remember praying the Rosary as a family. Our homes are the domestic church, and they can be houses of God for our family and friends.

One time I was spending a few days with my friend Mary Ann, also a Dominican sister, at her parent's rented beach house. All her sisters, their husbands, and nieces and nephews were playing games, watching TV, and happily conversing. Amid it all, when the clock struck 9:00 p.m., her Irish father, Michael, knelt next to the corner couch and began reciting his night prayers in a low voice. No one thought it unusual but me—it was part of ordinary life for this devoted Irish family. I was so taken by this sacred act in a beach house. Mr. Collins quietly and unconsciously witnessed his love for and devotion to God to his grandchildren and all present.

When I was in the third or fourth grade, my friend and neighbor, Melinda, invited me to her Congregational church picnic. The barbecue was fired up and the games had begun. When the food was ready to be served, the minister gathered us around the picnic table area. He spoke freely about God's love and presence in the gathered community and in the beautiful surrounding of the park. He spontaneously prayed a blessing over the food and all present. I was eight or nine years old at the time but remember being very touched by that prayer—it was so personal and intimate. I had never heard a Catholic pray that way. I remember talking to my mom about it, saying, "They really seem to know God like a friend. Can I go to that church sometime?" My mom responded, "We will see."

When I ministered in the South Bronx, there was a woman from the Caribbean named Beatrice. She always came dressed up for daily Mass and often wore a hat. Every day as we left the chapel, we would wish her a good day, and Beatrice would respond, "Be a blessing and walk with the king." Thirty-five years later, I remember her God-talk, and it still puts a smile on my face.

Another person I know who speaks freely about God is Bob Eid. He shared, "To me, talking about God is just talking about how I experience love in my everyday life." I got to know him and his wonderful wife, Carol, on a pilgrimage to Italy. One minute, Bob was teasing and cracking jokes with his buddy, Dominic; and in the next breath he was talking about God. He is a member of the early morning men's small Christian community at the Church of the Presentation in New Jersey. They meet weekly to pray, share faith, and support one another in living the Christian life. Small communities are sacred circles that help members to learn how to engage in God-talk, as Bob's example shows.

THE *Everyday Witness* OF *Bob Eid*

Bob is one of nine children, and a twin to boot. There are only ten years between the first and last of his siblings. You can imagine how lively that household was. His mom and dad were devout Catholics. His dad was a custodian in several Catholic churches in New Jersey. Bob shared with me that his father didn't make much money, but he always had faith that God would provide for his family. Before bedtime, they would all kneel at the couch in the living room and pray the Rosary together. God was a regular part of their everyday life.

Bob is a fun-loving guy who just makes me smile when I see him. He engages in God-talk in a way that is natural and rings true—no pious platitudes or warnings of damnation. Bob shared with me one of the many turning points along his faith journey, which brought him closer to God. It called him to minister to those who are suffering. He said, "The greatest gift God ever gave me was clinical depression, which I had after my second daughter was born. I lost the ability to love myself and thought I was the worst person in the world. I told my wife I did not love her or the girls. Finally, through God's grace and mercy, I recovered from that depression and was able to love myself and my family again. The pain and suffering from that episode gave me a compassionate heart. Whenever I see someone in emotional or physical pain, my heart goes out to that person, and I want them to feel the love that God has returned to my heart."

I asked him how he engages so easily in God-talk. He replied, "It is easy for me to talk about my faith because for me it is just talking about love, which everyone can relate to. I don't talk about doctrine or tell people they should go to church."

At one small Christian community leader's meeting, Bob had shared that his sister's mother-in-law, Joan, was dying alone in a nearby nursing home. Her family was fighting among themselves, and that night no one was with her. Bob said, "This woman [at the meeting], Marly, gave me a cross to bring to her and said a prayer as she gave me the cross. Well, the meeting ended at 10:00 p.m., and I said to myself, 'What am I going to do with this cross?' God put in my heart to go right to the nursing home and give Joan the cross. While there, I repeated Marly's prayer the best I could and left the cross in Joan's hands. In the morning, my sister texted me that Joan died later that night. I called her and asked if she had found a cross in the room. Crying, my sister said, "Bob, was that you who did that? You don't know what it meant to the family. She did not die alone."

I asked Bob if he had any recent experiences of talking about God, and he said, "Of course, yesterday." Bob had taken early retirement from IBM, and in addition to his many volunteer ministries, he works as a handyman. That day he was hired to put up curtain rods for a woman. As he was putting up the rods, he began talking to her. She shared with him that she just lost her dad. She said her dad used to hang the curtain rods and do all the work around the house. The woman began to talk about her loss, and it led into a spiritual conversation. As he began to share about his ministry to the sick, she told him about an experience she had a few years before, when her dad was in the hospital. Two women from the local parish brought her dad Communion, and during the simple service one of them asked if she and her sister also wanted to receive Communion. They were surprised, but said yes. The experience was healing and consoling for her and her family. It moved her to become an Extraordinary Minister of Holy Communion and bring Communion to the homebound. What could be more ordinary than engaging in God-talk while hanging a stranger's curtain rods?

Prompts FOR Self-Reflection

Jonathan Merritt, in his article "It's Getting Harder to Talk About God," highlights several reasons why Americans shy away from discussions about God or their faith. Which one most describes why you hesitate to have spiritual conversations?

Do you know someone who talks about spiritual things?
How can you learn from them?

Reflect on the last spiritual conversation you had with
someone.

Growing THE *Habit* OF *Engaging* IN *God-Talk*

Ask: Pray for the grace to engage in God-talk in a natural and unobtrusive way.

Be Aware: Notice when others talk about spiritual things, and note it. What words do they use? How did the conversation start? Who initiated it?

Be Intentional: Review the dos and don'ts of God-talk.

Be an Everyday Witness: Talk with someone about something you are grateful for, or share with someone a message you heard during the homily or something you read that was helpful to you.

Prayer TO *Engage* IN *God-Talk*

All-holy God, you are the one and true God.
Help me to love you with all my heart,
with all my soul, and with all my strength.
Keep these words in my heart today and every day.
Give me the grace to engage in God-talk,
with my family, with the children in my life,

and with all who need your message of love.
I pray this in the name of Jesus Christ, your Son,
who lives in union with you and the Holy Spirit,
now and forever.
Amen.

EPILOGUE

GO AND ANNOUNCE THE GOSPEL OF THE LORD

At the end of every Mass, we are sent forth into the world with a command. "Go forth, the Mass is ended." "Go and announce the Gospel of the Lord." "Go in peace, glorifying the Lord by your life." "Go in peace." Whichever dismissal is chosen, the emphasis is on the word *go*. More than a mere declaration that it is time to leave, the dismissal has the purpose of emphasizing our Christian call to mission. The word *Mass* comes from the Latin word *missa*, which is the root of the English word *mission*. At one time, people were dismissed with "*Ite, missa est*," which literally translates as "Go, be sent."

At the dismissal, we are grasped by the Spirit, our shoulders turned away from the altar and toward the doors of the church. We are sent into the street to be an everyday witness to Christ. We who have received Word and Eucharist are called, as St. Augustine reminds us, to become what we have received—the Body of Christ for others. For Christians, Sunday is not the end of the week, but the beginning. Every Sunday, we are transformed by our encounter with Christ, and we are sent on our two beautiful feet on a mission—to be everyday witnesses for the sake of the Church and the world.

Through our baptism, each of us is called to participate in the mission of Jesus. After Jesus' baptism, he entered the synagogue and proclaimed his mission with fire and focus: "The Spirit of the Lord is upon me, because he has anointed me to bring good news to the poor. He has sent me to proclaim release to the captives and recovery of sight to the blind, to let the oppressed go free, to proclaim the year of the Lord's favor" (Lk 4:18–19). The same Spirit that filled Jesus with fire and focus is the same Spirit that we have received at our baptism. Through our baptism we were incorporated into Christ and into the priesthood of believers. Our baptism calls us to extend to all the love, compassion, and mercy of God that we have come to know. We give expression to our baptismal reality by saying yes to becoming everyday witnesses.

I began this book with Pope Francis's definition of witness, "Christian witness is done with three things: words, the heart, and the hands." It is with all three that we go and announce the Gospel of the Lord. Like Jesus, we are to announce God's love and mercy to the materially poor, the poor in spirit, the stranger, the imprisoned, the sick in mind and body, and the oppressed. Everyday witnesses announce the God who is behind us, beside us, and in front of us—meeting us at every turn, in every bump in the road, and through every detour on our life journey. Everyday witnesses stand up for the dignity of every human life and the care of God's creation. Everyday witnesses announce the Good News and denounce injustice.

In his apostolic letter on everyday holiness, *Rejoice and Be Glad*, Pope Francis calls every baptized person to live holy lives in whatever they do. He names ordinary Christians who live holy lives the "saints next door." Francis writes, "Very often it is a holiness found in our next-door neighbors, those who, living in our midst, reflect God's presence. We might call them 'the middle class of holiness.'" Throughout this simple book I have shared stories about the "saints next door" and how they have reflected God's presence to me. We need to notice and share these God-stories of ordinary saints and everyday witnesses to inspire first ourselves and then others to become "saints next door" as well.

Though each of us is called to be an everyday witness, there are many ways to do it—we each do so in our own way. When we let God work through who we are, with the unique gifts we possess, we are most effective in revealing Christ to others. The call to be an everyday witness is a call to every Christian and not just to those with a special gift. The "how" of witness and "to whom" varies, but there are no excuses, for we are all called and sent.

Pray for and practice the seven habits explored in this book. Let them develop and grow in you according to your personality and gifts. Whatever our age or station in life, we are a work in progress—God's work. Be patient with yourself. You are fearfully and wonderfully made. Do you recall the big yellow button I told you about that read, "God Does Not Make Junk"? God needs you, with your warts and all, to announce an alternative way, Jesus' way, by sharing your faith by your words, your heart, and your hands. Go and announce the Gospel of the Lord! Go in peace, glorifying the Lord by your life!

PRACTICAL IDEAS FOR YOU AND YOUR PARISH

Tips FOR *Sharing* YOUR *Faith Story*

First, think about your personal faith journey, and ask the Holy Spirit to guide you as you reflect on these questions:

- How did this journey start when you were young, and how did it change as you moved into adulthood?
- What were the key moments or turning points?

- Did you lose your faith? Did you have doubts?
- When did you recognize God's love in something that happened to you?
- What person or event in your life served as a catalyst?
- What happened to your faith as a result?

Then, here are a few tips for when you share your story or give a witness talk:

- Tell one story.
- Describe your God-moment with the necessary detail.
- Share only experiences that you have worked through.
- Don't be the hero or heroine of the story.
- Write it out as you would tell it out loud.
- Look at the people you are speaking to, and ask for the grace to love them.

Tips FOR Cultivating A Sense OF Witnessing TO Faith IN YOUR Parish

Consider implementing some of these ideas:

- Provide opportunities for people to give witness to their faith at different parish events.
- Invite parishioners to give live or video faith witness stories at the beginning or end of Mass or at other appropriate occasions.
- Gather the faith stories and publish them.
- Make short video clips with the faith stories; post them on social media.
- Establish small faith-sharing groups in your parish to increase a sense of belonging and to form everyday witnesses to faith.
- Incorporate faith sharing into all parish meetings.
- Plan for the public faith witness of the whole parish through activities such as a food pantry or gratis meal, participation in local parades and fairs, or outreach to other religious communities in the parish boundaries. Tell the story through publicity in local media, social media, and direct mail contact.

- Conduct a door-to-door campaign to introduce your parish community to the people who live in your boundaries. Acquaint people with the parish's programs and outreach, and leave door hangers with this information for those not home. Invite parishioners to witness to their faith and how the parish accompanies them in their faith journey.

Adapted from Be My Witness: Formation for the New Evangelization, © *RENEW International. Used with permission.*

THERESA RICKARD, O.P., is a Dominican Sister of Blauvelt, New York, a well-known retreat leader, and the president of RENEW International. She is the author of *Daily Devotions for Advent 2015*, *Daily Devotions for Lent 2014*, and *LiveLent!* Rickard also contributed to *Preaching the Sunday Assembly* and *We Preach Christ Crucified*.

She earned a doctorate of ministry in preaching from Aquinas Institute of Theology in St. Louis, Missouri, a master of divinity degree from Union Theological Seminary in New York City, and a master of arts degree in religion and religious education at Fordham University.

Prior to working at RENEW, Rickard ministered in two multicultural parishes in the South Bronx, was the director of vocation and formation ministry for her congregation, and was a member of the Archdiocese of New York's Parish Mission Team.

www.renewintl.org
Facebook: RENEWIntl
Twitter: @RENEWIntl